www.donbousquet.com

QuahogMaid Books
18 Namcook Road
Narragansett, RI 02882-2222

To order books call:
Office Emporium (401) 782-3930, or
www.donbousquet.com

ISBN: 0-9713584-2-7
First Edition
10 9 8 7 6 5 4 3

MY RHODE ISLAND

Okay, so it's not really "MY" Rhode Island. As of this writing it actually belongs to the Speaker of the House of the Rhode Island Legislature. But that's another story.

When I graduated from the University of Rhode Island with a degree in anthropology, it was time to go out and do some fieldwork. To an anthropologist this means traveling to exotic places to record the daily lives of strikingly unusual people. So I did that. I put on a three-piece suit and got a job in Providence.

My new position involved driving all over Rhode Island to "develop relationships with other businesses" for my company. This activity got me into every city, town and hamlet in the State of Rhode Island. I was then able to employ the participant/observer technique that is central to cultural anthropology fieldwork. My three-piece camouflage worked perfectly. I'm sure none of the natives had any idea they had an anthropologist in their midst. I researched every detail, every nuance of their lives--the bizarre foods they ate, the odd form of the English language they spoke in a dozen or more dialects which are almost unintelligible to other Homo sapiens. I surreptitiously acquired this information, and more, over a six-year term.

Since 1982 I have been publishing the results of my fieldwork in the form of "cartoon collections." This is the eighteenth book. My Rhode Island means a lot of different things to me. But, mostly, my Rhode Island is funny.

Don Bousquet
Bonnet Shores
May, 2003

THE AUTHOR
IN THE FIELD
CA. 1978

2

RHODE ISLANDER ABOUT
TO MAKE A RIGHT TURN.

Don Bousquet

5

PONY RIDES $1.⁰⁰

Don Bousquet

WHEN I GROW UP, I WANNA BE A WAITER AT 'HOOTERS'!!
DON BOUSQUET
NOT THE SHARPEST KNIFE IN THE DRAWER

11

14

15

17

19

MUST BE A TURKEY
BUZZARD OR SOMETHIN'
'CAUSE THIS THING
IS HUGE !!

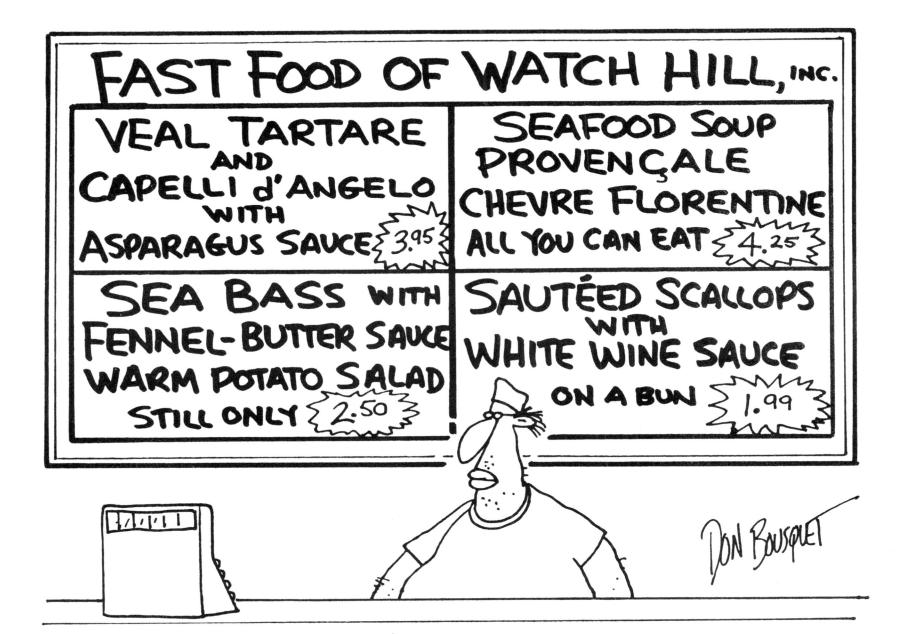

23

24

I CAN REMEMBER
HAVING A LONGER NECK.
I USED TO BE ABLE
TO SEE MY FEET.
DON BOUSQUET

THE NEW INDEPENDENT MAN
HIGH ATOP THE STATE HOUSE

HEATED MIRRORS

Don Bousquet

28

WELCOME TO RHODE ISLANDERS HEAVEN

ROCKY PT. PARK

SHEPARD'S TEA ROOM

"THE TENT"

AMERICA'S CUP RACE

NARRAGANSETT CASINO

SALTY BRINE'S SHACK

CRESCENT PARK

33

37

BE CAREFUL WHAT YOU WISH FOR—
YOU JUST MIGHT GET IT.

J.J. CURZIO OF
EAST GREENWICH
ALWAYS WANTED
TO BE A
BABE
MAGNET.

DON BOUSQUET

GEORGIA
ON MY MIND

FIFTY-THREE YEARS AGO WE GOT MARRIED IN PAWTUCKET BUT HE WANTED TO WAKE UP IN A CITY THAT NEVER SLEEPS SO WE MOVED TO ATTLEBORO.

43

44

45

TRANSPLANTED RHODE ISLANDERS

49

51

57

...AND HOW COOL IS THIS BABY? SHE'S GOT REMOTE ENTRY, CUP HOLDERS AND A MOONROOF!!
DON BOUSQUET

60

61

64

OCEAN STATE SYMPATHY CARDS

VISIT TO REGISTRY

LOST SHIRT AT CASINO

SEPTIC SYSTEM FAILED

MAYOR IN SLAMMER

Don Bousquet

DOG HEAVEN

NEGATIVE CAMPAIGNING

OH, SHOOWA, I CAN TAWK NOW. AHM JUS' DOIN' THE LONDREE AN' LISTENIN' TA AHHLENE VYELITT.

Don Bousquet

74

75

BUDGET LAP POOL

Don Bousquet

77

79

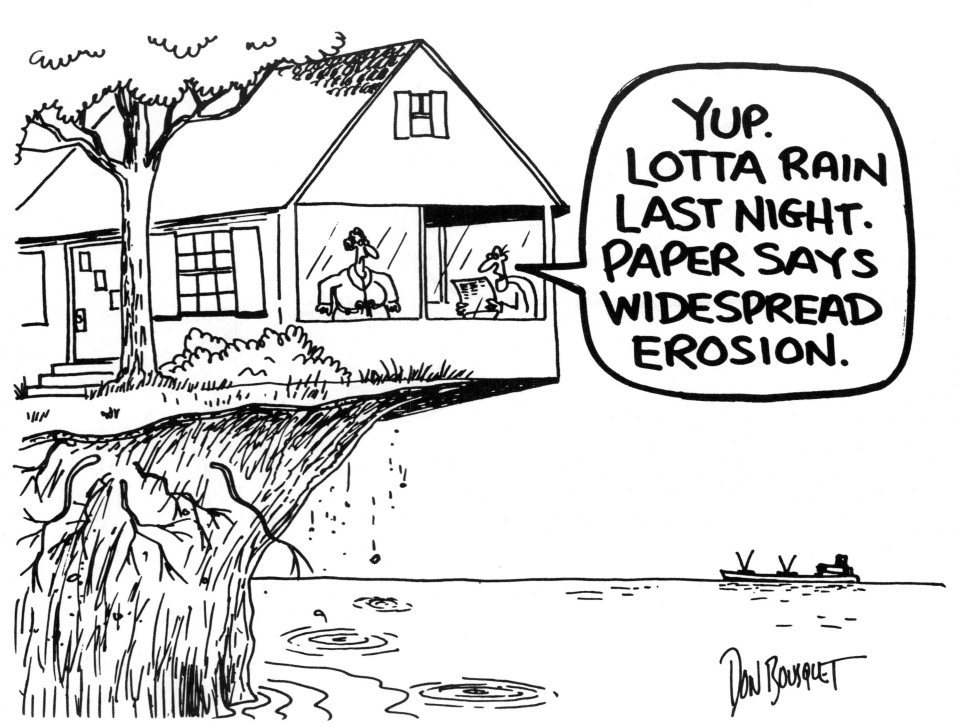

85

87

89

94

97

A RHODE ISLAND D.O.T. OFFICIAL AND HIS CRUMBLING INFRASTRUCTURE